D0071719

1

<u>Planning My Escape:</u>

Comprehensive Safety Plan
for
Victims & Survivors
of
Domestic Violence

After The Trauma, Inc 2021

Planning My Escape: **REVISED**
Safety Plan for Victims/Survivors of Domestic Violence

The Hardest Decision

Planning to leave an abusive relationship is the hardest decision to make. So many things to take into consideration (where will you go, legal steps, uprooting children, explaining to others, etc). Others may feel that your reasons for leaving are not valid. Just because you don't have physical scars doesn't mean you are not a victim or survivor. 80% of victims/survivors don't have physical scars to prove their abuse.

When you are in this type of situation, it is very important that you understand that **NO ONE** understands your condition better than you. They are not there with you when the abuse takes place. There isn't any way of knowing what your abuser will do next. Therefore, you are the best person to make this decision.

A safety plan is one of the best tools you can have when trying to come to the best decision for you and your children or for yourself. The safety plan, in the book, is a comprehensive, step-by-step plan to assist you in eight areas of your life. All you have to do is fill in the blanks. **DO NOT** take this plan home. Leave it at your office or give it to a trusted friend or relative. As a matter of fact, only tell one person (a trusted friend or relative) what you intend to do. Any more than one will hamper your efforts to leave, because you don't know who your abuser knows. And once the abuser knows, your plan is out the window.

After The Trauma, Inc 2021

Leaving an abusive relationship is the most dangerous time for you. Why? Because the abuser will feel that the control is no longer there. Which makes the abuser a very dangerous person and all rational is non-existent. Leaving is also hard because you begin the remember the loving time in that relationship and of the many years you have put into it. Then the thoughts of 'how did we get here' will surface.

Listen, **YOU** know your abuser better than anyone. Rely on what you know and use it to your benefit. Follow your spirit, it will not lead you astray. Pray and ask God for guidance. Ask Him to put people and resources in place to help you.

Only **YOU** will know when it is time to leave. Don't be so concerned with what your abuser is feeling that you stop caring about your safety. Always remember, it is NOT your fault and it is never too late to stand up for yourself. However, be wise, strategic, and careful.

The 24-hour National Hotline for Domestic Violence

800-799-SAFE (7233)

It's time to go....

<u>Planning for Safety</u>

A safety plan is a must have in a domestic violence situation. Victims/Survivors will need to plan a strategic safety route that will allow them to leave without incident. Just remember, leaving is the most dangerous time, so be careful!

Please share this plan with **<u>ANYONE</u>** that need information on what to do in a domestic violence situation for the safety of their lives and the lives of their children.

After The Trauma, Inc 2021

PERSONALIZED SAFETY PLAN

The following steps represent my plan for increasing my safety and preparing in advance for the possibility for further violence. Although I do not have control over my partner's violence, I do have a choice about how to respond to him/her and how to maneuver myself and my children to safety.

STEP 1: *Safety during a violent incident.*

Women cannot always avoid violent incidents. To increase safety, a variety of strategies can be used.

I can use some or all the following strategies:

    A. If I decide to leave, I will _____
_____. (*Practice how to get out safely. Analyze which doors, windows, elevators, stairwells, or fire escapes would you use?*)

    B. I can keep my purse and car keys ready and put them (*location*) _____ to leave quickly.

    C. I can inform _____ about the violence and request they call the police if they hear suspicious noises coming from my house.

    D. I can teach my children how to use the telephone to contact the police and the fire department.

After The Trauma, Inc 2021

E. I will use _____ as my code word with my children and my friends so they can call for help.

F. If I must leave my home, I will go _____ _____. (*Decide this even*

if you don't think there will be a next time.) If I cannot go to the location above, then I can go to

_____ or _____.

G. I can also teach some of these strategies to my children.

H.   When I expect we are going to have an argument, I will try to move to a space that is lowest risk, such as _____. (*Avoid arguments in the bathroom, garage, kitchens, near weapons or in rooms without access to an outside door.*)

I. I will be confident using my judgment and intuition. If the situation is very serious, I can give my partner what he/she wants to calm him/her down. I must protect myself until I/we are out of danger.

After The Trauma, Inc 2021

<u>STEP 2:</u> *Safety when preparing to leave.*

Abused women frequently leave the residence they share with the abuser. Leaving must be done with a careful plan in order to increase safety. Abusers often strike back when they believe the victim is leaving their relationship.

I can use some or all the following safety strategies:

    A. I will leave money and an extra set of keys with __
           _____ so I can leave quickly.

    B. I will keep copies of important documents or keys at

        _____.

    C. I will open a savings account by _____
        _____ to increase my independence.

Other things I can do to increase my independence include:

_____

_____

_____

_____.

    D. The domestic violence program's hotline number is
        _____**800-799-7233**_____. My local
        coalition phone number is _____
        _____. I can seek shelter by
        calling both numbers.

                           After The Trauma, Inc 2021

E. I will purchase a TRAC phone for emergency calls to the hotline and police. This will ensure that my telephone communications are confidential because my abuser will not have access to my data.

F. I will check with _____ and _____ _____ to see who would be able to let me stay with them or lend me money.

G. I can leave extra clothing with _____ _____ as well as hide 3 days of clothing in my trunk.

H. I will review my safety plan every _____ in order to plan the safest way to leave my residence. _____ (*Domestic violence advocate or friend*) has agreed to help me review this plan.

I. I will rehearse my escape plan with my children.

Notes: _____

_____

_____

_____

_____

_____

_____

_____

After The Trauma, Inc 2021

<u>STEP 3:</u> *Safety in my own residence.*

There are many things that a woman can do to increase her safety in her own residence. It may be impossible to do everything at once, but safety measures can be added step by step.

<u>Safety measures I can use include:</u>

A.   I can change the locks on my doors and windows as soon as possible.

B.   I can replace wooden doors (*if necessary*) with steel/metal doors.

C.   I can install security systems including additional locks, window bars, poles to sedge against doors, an electronic system, etc.

D.   I can purchase rope ladders to be used for escape from higher floor windows.

E.   I can install smoke detectors and purchase fire extinguishers for each floor in my house/apartment.

F.   I can install an outside lighting system that lights up when a person is coming close to my house.

G.   I will teach my children how to use the phone to make a call to _____(friend/minister/other) for help.

After The Trauma, Inc 2021

STEP 4: *Safety with a protection order*

Many abusers obey protection orders, but one can never be sure which violent partner will obey and which will violate protection orders.

The following are some steps that I can take to help the enforcement of my protection order:

A. I will always keep my protection order near me. (*Always keep it on or near your person. If you change purses, that's the first thing that should go in.*)

B. I will give my protection order to police departments in the community where I work, in those communities where I usually visit family or friends, and in the community where I live.

C. There should be a county/parish registry of protection orders that all police departments can call to confirm a protection order. I can check to make sure that my order is in the registry. The phone number for the county registry of protection orders is _____. (*Register protective order at the courthouse under Full, Faith & Credit.*)

D. For further safety, if I often visit other counties/parishes, I might file my protection order with the court in those counties/parishes. I will register my protection order in the following counties/parishes:
_____ and _____.

After The Trauma, Inc 2021

E.   I can call the local domestic violence program if I am not sure about B., C., or D. above or if I have some problem with my protection order.

F.   I will inform my employer, my minister, my closest friend that I have a protection order in effect.

G.   If my partner destroys my protection order, I can get another copy from the courthouse.

H.   If my partner violates the protection order, I can call the police and report a violation, contact my attorney, call my advocate, and/or advise the court of the violation.

I.   If the police do not help, I can contact my advocate or attorney and will file a complaint with the Chief of the police department.

J.   I can also file a private criminal complaint in the jurisdiction where the violation occurred or with the district attorney. I can charge my abuser with a violation of the protection order and all the crimes that he commits in violating the order. I can call a domestic violence advocate to help me.

Notes: _____

_____

_____

_____

_____

After The Trauma, Inc 2021

STEP 5: *Safety on the job and in public.*

Every abused woman must decide when she will tell others that her partner has abused her and that she may be at continued risk. Friends, family and co-workers can help to protect women. Each woman should consider carefully which people to invite to help secure her safety.

I might do any or all the following:

A.   I can inform my supervisor and the security supervisor at work of my situation.

B.   I can ask _____ to help screen my telephone calls to work.

C.   When leaving work, I can _____
_____ _____
_____.

D.   When driving home, if problems occur, I can _____
_____
_____.

E.   If I use public transportation, I can _____
_____
_____
_____.

F.   I can use different grocery stores and shopping malls for shopping.

    After The Trauma, Inc 2021

G.   I can use a different bank and take care of my banking at hours different from those I used when residing with my battering partner.

H.   I can also _____

_____

_____ .

Notes: _____

_____

_____

_____

_____

_____

_____

_____

_____

_____

_____

_____

_____

_____

<u>STEP 6</u>:   *Safety and drug or alcohol use.*

Most people in this culture use alcohol. Many use mood-altering drugs. Much of this use is legal and some is not. The legal outcomes of using illegal drugs can be very hard on the victim and may hurt her relationship with her children as well as put her at a disadvantage in other legal actions with her abuser.

Therefore, victims should carefully consider the potential cost of the use of illegal drugs. But beyond this, the use of any alcohol or other drugs can reduce a woman's awareness and ability to act quickly to protect herself from her abuser. Furthermore, the use of alcohol or other drugs by the abuser may give him/her an excuse to use violence. Therefore, in the context of drug or alcohol use, a victim needs to make specific safety plans.

If drug or alcohol use has occurred in my relationship, I can enhance my safety by the following:

A.   If I am going to use, I can do so in a safe place and with people who understand the risk of violence and are committed to my safety.

B.   I can also _____

_____

_____ .

C.   If my partner is using, I can _____ .

_____

_____ .

D.   I might also _____

_____

_____ .

E.   To safeguard my children, I might _____

_____ and

_____ .

Notes: _____

_____

_____

_____

_____

_____

_____

_____

_____

_____

_____

_____

_____

After The Trauma, Inc 2021

STEP 7: *Safety and my emotional health*

The experience of being physically and verbally degraded by abusers is usually exhausting and emotionally draining. The process of building a new life for myself takes much courage and incredible energy.

To conserve my emotional energy, resources AND to avoid hard emotional times, I can do some of the following:

A.   If I feel down and ready to return to a potentially abusive situation, I can _____

_____

_____

_____.

B.

When I must communicate with my partner in person or by telephone, I can _____.

C.   I can tell myself "_____

_____"whenever I feel others are trying to control or abuse me.

D.   I can call _____ and _____ to help me feel stronger.

E.   Other things I can do to help me feel stronger are _____and _____

_____.

After The Trauma, Inc 2021

F.   I can attend workshops and support groups at the domestic violence program or _____ _____, _____ _____, or _____ to gain support and strengthen my relationships with other people.

Notes: _____

_____

_____

_____

_____

_____

_____

_____

_____

_____

_____

_____

_____

_____

_____

_____

_____

After The Trauma, Inc 2021

STEP 8: *Items to take when leaving*

When victims leave abusers, it is important to take certain items with them. Beyond this, victims should give an extra copy of protective orders and an extra set of clothing to a friend just in case they must leave quickly.

✓ Items with a check mark listed below are the most important to take with you. If there is time, the other items might be taken, or stored outside the home.

These items are to be placed in one location, so that if we must leave in a hurry, they can grab them quickly.

When I leave, I should take:

✓ Identification for myself and child(ren)
✓ Lease/rental agreement & payment history
✓ Children's birth certificates
✓ Insurance information
✓ Birth certificates
✓ Pictures
✓ Social security cards
✓ Jewelry
✓ School and vaccination records
✓ Children's favorite toy(s)/blanket(s)
✓ Money
✓ Items of sentimental value
✓ Checkbook, ATM card
✓ Credit cards

After The Trauma, Inc 2021

- ✓ Keys – house/car/office
- ✓ Driver's license and registration
- ✓ Medications
- ✓ Passport(s)
  Welfare identification
  Work permits
  Green card
  Divorce papers
  Medical records – for all family members

Notes: _____

_____

_____

_____

_____

_____

_____

_____

_____

_____

_____

Emergency Telephone numbers list in my phone:

Police department – home _____

Police department – school _____

Police department – work _____

Battered women's program _____

Battered men's program _____

County/Parish registry of protection orders _____

Work number _____

Supervisor's home number _____

Minister _____

Others _____

After The Trauma, Inc 2021

State Coalitions Against Domestic Violence List

Locate the one in your state and call for help!

You are not alone!

After The Trauma, Inc 2021

Find a coalition in your area. They are there to help!

 After The Trauma, Inc 2021

Alabama Coalition Against
Domestic Violence
(334) 832-4842.
Fax: (334) 832-4803
(800) 650-6522 Hotline
Website: www.acadv.org
Email:
info@aca
dv.org

Alaska Network on Domestic
and Sexual Violence
(907) 586-3650
Fax: (907) 463-4493
Website: www.andvsa.org
Email: andvsa@andvsa.org

Arizona Coalition Against
Domestic Violence
(602) 279-2900
Fax: (602) 279-2980
(800) 782-6400 Nationwide
Website: www.azcadv.org
Email: info@azadv.org

Arkansas Coalition Against
Domestic Violence
(501) 907-5612
Fax: (501) 907-5618
(800) 269-4668 Nationwide
Website:
www.domesticpeace.com
Email:
acadv@domesticpeace.com

California Partnership to End
Domestic Violence
(916) 444-7163
Fax: (916) 444-7165
(800) 524-4765 Nationwide
Website: www.cpedv.org
Email: info@cpedv.org

Colorado Coalition Against
Domestic Violence
(303) 831-9632
Fax: (303) 832-7067
(888) 788-7091
Website: www.ccadv.org
Email: info@ccadv.org

Connecticut Coalition Against
Domestic Violence
(860) 282-7899
Fax: (860) 282-7892
(800) 281-1481 In State
(888) 774-2900 In State DV
Hotline
Website: www.ctcadv.org
Email: contactus@ctcadv.org

Delaware Coalition Against
Domestic Violence
(302) 658-2958
Fax: (302) 658-5049
(800) 701-0456 Statewide
Website: www.dcadv.org
Email: dcadvadmin@dcadv.org

DC Coalition Against Domestic
Violence
(202) 299-1181
Fax: (202) 299-1193
Website: www.dccadv.org
Email: info@dccadv.org

Florida Coalition Against
Domestic Violence
(850) 425-2749
Fax: (850) 425-3091
(850) 621-4202 TDD
(800) 500-1119 In State
Website: www.fcadv.org

Georgia Coalition Against
Domestic Violence
(404) 209-0280
Fax: (404) 766-3800
Crisis Line (800)334-2836
Website: www.gcadv.org
Email: info@gcadv.org

Hawaii State Coalition Against
Domestic Violence
(808) 832-9316
Fax: (808) 841-6028
Website: www.hscadv.org
Email: admin@hscadv.org

Idaho Coalition Against Sexual
& Domestic Violence
(208) 384-0419
Fax: (208) 331-0687
(888) 293-6118 Nationwide
Website: www.idvsa.org
Email: info@engagingvoices.org

Illinois Coalition Against
Domestic Violence
(217) 789-2830
Fax: (217) 789-1939
Website: www.ilcadv.org
Email: ilcadv@ilcadv.org

Indiana Coalition Against
Domestic Violence
(317) 917-3685
Fax: (317) 917-3695
(800) 332-7385 In State
Website:
www.violenceresource.org
Email:
icadv@violenceresource.org

Iowa Coalition against Domestic
Violence
(515) 244-8028
Fax: (515) 244-7417
(800) 942-0333 In State
Hotline
Website: www.icadv.org,
Email: icadv@icadv.org

Kansas Coalition against Sexual
and Domestic Violence
(785) 232-9784
Fax: (785) 266-1874
Website: www.kcsdv.org
Email: coalition@kcsdv.org

Kentucky Domestic Violence
Association
(502) 209-5382
Fax: (502) 226-5382
Website: www.kdva.org
Email: info@kdva.org

Louisiana Coalition Against
Domestic Violence
(225) 752-1296
Fax: (225) 751-8927
Website: www.lcadv.org;
Email: info@icadv.org

Maine Coalition to End
Domestic Violence
(207) 430-8334
Fax: (207) 430-8348
Website: www.mcedv.org
Email: info@mcedv.org

Maryland Network Against
Domestic Violence
(301) 429-3601
Fax: (301) 809-0422
(800) 634-3577 Nationwide
Website: www.mnadv.org
Email: info@mnadv.org

Jane Doe, Inc./Massachusetts
Coalition Against Sexual Assault
and Domestic Violence
(617) 248-0922
Fax: (617) 248-0902
TTY/TTD: (617) 263-2200
Website: www.janedoe.org
Email: info@janedoe.org

Michigan Coalition against
Domestic & Sexual Violence
(517) 347-7000
Fax/TTY: (517) 240-0902
Website: www.mcadsv.org
Email: general@mcadsv.org

Minnesota Coalition for
Battered Women
(651) 646-6177
Fax: (651) 646-1527
Crisis Line: (651) 646-0994
(800) 289-6177 Nationwide
Website: www.mcbw.org
Email: mcbw@mcbw.org

Mississippi Coalition Against
Domestic Violence
(601) 981-9196
Fax: (601) 981-2501
(800) 898-3234
Website: www.mcadv.org
Email: support@mcadv.org

Missouri Coalition Against
Domestic Violence
(573) 634-4161
Fax: (573) 636-3728
Website: www.mocadsv.org
Email: mocadsv@mocadsv.org

Montana Coalition Against
Domestic & Sexual Violence
(406) 443-7794
Fax: (406) 443-7818
(888) 404-7794 Nationwide
Website: www.mcadsv.com
Email: mtcoalition@mcadsv.com

Nebraska Domestic Violence
and Sexual Assault Coalition
(402) 476-6256
Fax: (402) 476-6806
(800) 876-6238 In State
Hotline
(877) 215-0167 Spanish
Hotline
Website: www.ndvsac.org
Email: help@ndvsac.org

Nevada Network Against
Domestic Violence
(775) 828-1115
Fax: (775) 828-9911
Website: www.nnadv.org
Email: info@nnadv.org

New Hampshire Coalition
Against Domestic and Sexual
Violence

(603) 224-8893; Fax: (603)
228-6096 (866) 644-3574 In
State

Website: www.nhcadsv.org
Email: info@nhcadsv.org

New Jersey Coalition for
Battered Women
(609) 584-8107
Fax: (609) 584-9750
(800) 572-7233 In State
Website: www.njcbw.org
Email: info@njcbw.org

New Mexico State Coalition
Against Domestic Violence
(505) 246-9240
Fax: (505) 246-9434
(800) 773-3645 In State
Website: www.nmcadv.org;
Email: info@nmcadv.org

New York State Coalition
Against Domestic Violence
(518) 482-5464
Fax: (518) 482-3807
(800) 942-5465 English-In
State
(800) 942-6908 Spanish-In
State
Website: www.nyscadv.org
Email: nyscadv@nyscadv.org

North Carolina Coalition
Against Domestic Violence
(919) 956-9124
Fax: (919) 682-1449
(888) 997-9124 Nation wide
Website: www.nccadv.org

North Dakota Council on
Abused Women's Services
(701) 255-6240
Fax: (701) 255-1904
(888) 255-6240 Nationwide
Website: www.ndcaws.org
Email:
contact@cawsnorthdakota.org

Action Ohio Coalition for
Battered Women
(614) 825-0551
Fax: (614) 825-0673
(888) 622-9315 In State
Website: www.actionohio.org
Email: actionohio@wowway.biz

Ohio Domestic Violence
Network
(614) 781-9651
Fax: (614) 781-9652
(800) 934-9840
Website: www.odvn.org
Email: info@odvn.org

Oklahoma Coalition Against
Domestic Violence and Sexual
Assault
(405) 524-0700
Fax: (405) 524-0711
Website: www.ocadvsa.org
Email: Prevention@ocadvsa.org

Oregon Coalition Against
Domestic and Sexual Violence
(503) 230-1951
Fax: (503) 230-1973
Website: www.ocadsv.com
Email: adminasst@ocadsv.com

Pennsylvania Coalition Against
Domestic Violence
(717) 545-6400
Fax: (717) 545-9456
(800) 932-4632 Nationwide
Website: www.pcadv.org

The Office of Women
Advocates
(787) 721-7676; Fax: (787)
725-9248

Rhode Island Coalition Against
Domestic Violence
(401) 467-9940
Fax: (401) 467-9943
(800) 494-8100 In State
Website: www.ricadv.org
Email: ricadv@ricadv.org

South Carolina Coalition
Against Domestic Violence and
Sexual Assault
(803) 256-2900
Fax: (803) 256-1030
(800) 260-9293 Nationwide
Website: www.sccadvasa.org

South Dakota Coalition Against
Domestic Violence & Sexual
Assault
(605) 945-0869
Fax: (605) 945-0870
(800) 572-9196 Nationwide
Website:
www.southdakotacoalition.org
Email: SKing@sdcedsv.org

Tennessee Coalition Against
Domestic and Sexual Violence
(615) 386-9406
Fax: (615) 383-2967
(800) 289-
9018 In
State.
Website:
https://tncoalition.
org/
Email: tcadsv@tcadsv.org

Texas Council on Family
Violence
(512) 794-1133
Fax: (512) 794-1199
(800) 525-1978 In State
Website: www.tcfv.org

Utah Domestic Violence
Council
(801) 521-5544
Fax: (801) 521-5548
Website: www.udvac.org

Vermont Network Against
Domestic Violence and Sexual
Assault
(802)223-1302
Fax: (802) 223-6943.
(802) 223-1115 TTY
Website: www.vtnetwork.org
Email:
vtnetwork@vtnetwork.org

Virgin Island Domestic
Violence and Sexual Assault
Council
(340) 719-0144
Fax: (340) 719-5521
Website: www.vidvsac.org
Email: info@vidvsac.org

Virginia Sexual & Domestic
Violence Action Alliance
(804) 377-0335
Fax: (804) 377-0339
(800) 838-8238 Nationwide
Website: www.vsdvalliance.org
Email: info@vsdvalliance.org

Washington State Coalition
Against Domestic Violence
(360) 586-1022
Fax: (360) 586-1024
(360) 586-1029 TTY
&
(206) 389-2515
Fax. (206) 389-2520
(800) 886-2880 In State
(206)389-2900 TTY
Website: www.wscadv.org
Email: wscadv@wscadv.org

Washington State Native
American Coalition Against
Domestic & Sexual Assault
(360) 352-3120
Fax: (360) 357-3858
(888) 352-3120
Website: www.womenspirit.net
West Virginia Coalition Against
Domestic Violence
(304) 965-3552
Fax: (304) 965-3572
Website: www.wvcadv.org
Email: website@wvcadv.org

End Domestic Abuse
Wisconsin: The Wisconsin
Coalition Against Domestic
Violence
(608) 255-0539
Fax: (608) 255-3560
Website: www.endabusewi.org
Email: wcadv@wcadv.org

Wyoming Coalition Against
Domestic Violence and
Sexual Assault
(307) 755-5481
Fax: (307) 755-5482
(800) 990-3877 Nationwide
Website: www.wyomingdvsa.org
Email:
Info@mail.wyomingdvsa.org

****

Organizations providing assistance to victims/survivors

National Hotline for Domestic
Violence ~ 24- Hour Hotline
800-799-SAFE (7233)
TTY 800-787-3224

National Resource Center on Domestic
Violence
https://www.nrcdv.org/

Love is Respect – the National Dating Abuse
Helpline
866-331-9474
TTY 866-331-8453
Text "loveis" to 22522
Live chat at
https://www.loveisrespect.org/

Strong Hearts Native Helpline
844-762-8483
https://www.strongheartshelpline.org/

For rape/sexual assault services, contact
RAINN—the Rape Abuse Incest National
Network
800-656-4673 (HOPE)
Secure, online private chat:
https://hotline.rainn.org/online

Help for Men Who Are Being Abused
https://www.helpguide.org/articles/abuse/help-for-men-who-are-being-abused.htm

Domestic Shelters
https://www.domesticshelters.org/

FAMILY AND YOUTH SERVICES BUREAU
An Office of the Administration for Children & Families
https://www.acf.hhs.gov/fysb/programs/family-violence-prevention-services/programs/ndvh

Stalking Resource Center
www.ncvc.org

Notes: _____

_____

_____

_____

_____

_____

_____

_____

_____

_____

_____

_____

_____

_____

_____

_____

_____

_____

VINE ~ Victim Information & Notification Everyday

VINE Link is the online version of VINE (*Victim Information and Notification Everyday*), the National Victim Notification Network. This service allows crime victims to obtain timely and reliable information about criminal cases and the custody status of offenders 24 hours a day.

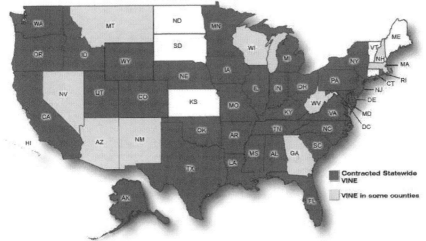

Victims and other concerned citizens can also register to be notified by phone, email or TTY device when an offender's custody status changes by visiting VINE Link at www.vinelink.com. Users can also register through their participating state or county toll-free number.

Contact Information:

(866-277-7477) or info@apprisssafety.com

You can also learn more about VINE at www.apprisssafety.com

©After the Trauma, Inc2021

VINE Link Web Site

Also, log onto **www.vinelink.com** for more information.

Put VINE to Work for You

For more information about VINE or to arrange for a demonstration,
contact Appriss at 1-866Appriss

Benefits Of VINE

Around-the-clock support — a staff of live operators to assist victims and technicians who monitor all VINE systems

- Saves taxpayers money by eliminating the need to manually notify victims, allowing staff to focus on their core responsibilities
- Provides life-saving services to victims at no cost
- Helps satisfy most states' legislative requirement for victim notification
- Depending on the community, victims can interface with VINE in multiple languages

- VINE generates about 700,000 notification calls each month

Where Is VINE?

- More than 2,100 communities nationwide
- Most of the nation's largest metropolitan areas
- More than two-thirds of the nation's Departments of Correction

- To date, more than two-thirds of the nation is using the patented VINE system to keep victims informed about offenders.
- All these communities are connected to the Appriss Data Network™, the nation's largest integrated criminal justice information database.
- Data from county and state prisons is collected by this central hub, where Appriss manages automated interfaces and monitors 13 million offender transactions each month.

How VINE Works

- VINE communicates with jail and prison booking systems in near real-time, transmitting updated information to the Appriss Data Network.
- Crime victims and the public can access the information by calling a local tollfree number, or logging onto www.vinelink.com, any time of the day or night.
- Victims can inquire whether an offender is held in jail as well as the facility's location.
- Users can register to be notified immediately of a change in the offender's status, such as release, transfer, or escape.
- When a notification is triggered, VINE automatically calls the number or numbers the victim has provided.
  - Calls continue for a designated period, or until the victim enters a four-digit PIN.

International Domestic Violence Resources

These are International Domestic Violence Resources
https://vachss.com/help_text/domestic_violence_intl.html

Notes: _____

_____

_____

_____

_____

_____

_____

_____

_____

_____

_____

_____

_____

_____

_____

_____

_____

_____

Made in the USA
Las Vegas, NV
15 September 2022

55325327R00024